No Sweat!

....

The Indispensable Guide to Reports and Dissertations

Ray Irving & Cathy Smith

....

89835 · IRL
001.4
7 day loan
research only

Copyright © Institute of Management Foundation

First published 1998

The Institute of Management
Management House
Cottingham Road
Corby
Northants NN17 1TT

British Library Cataloguing in Publication Data

A CIP catalogue record for this book is available from the
British Library

ISBN: 0-85946-295-1

Foreword

The importance of communication in business and management must not be underestimated. A key aspect of communication is report writing, and it is vital that we have clear ideas about how to make our reports effective.

This Guide is designed to help with just that - to assist you, the report or dissertation writer, to:

- deal with a complex topic
- address a given, often diverse, readership
- produce a document that is clear and unambiguous
- provoke a reaction.

It also gives advice on the earlier stages of the project, such as the selection of your subject, planning your time and carrying out research.

Your final dissertation will be read by many people - managers, team members, tutors, supervisors and external examiners - with interest. It will be stored and read by others in future years and, therefore, must be able to stand the test of public scrutiny.

It will be a major part of your award; so it is a task that cannot be undertaken without care and application. By following this Guide, the task will be made more palatable, and your learning will be enhanced - leading to a competence which is eminently transferable as you progress in your career.

Since you are reading this, your project is imminent - I commend this Guide to you and I wish you every success.

Professor Neville D Harris
Chief External Verifier, Institute of Management

January 1998

Contents

Introduction 1

1. What Makes an Outstanding Report or Dissertation? 3

Getting Started
2. Choosing a Subject 11
3. Planning the Project 21

Doing the Research
4. Desk Research and the Literature Review 31
5. Questionnaires and Sampling 39
6. Interviews and Observation 51
7. Case Studies 57

Bringing it all Together
8. Analysing your Results 61
9. Writing it up 69

And Finally 79

Appendices
Appendix 1 - References and Citations 83
Appendix 2 - Finding Information on Management 93
Appendix 3 - Finding Market and Company Information 97
Appendix 4 - Sources of Information on the Internet 103
Appendix 5 - Professional Associations in the Management Field 107

Introduction

What are the reasons for writing a report or dissertation?

Apart from the obvious answer of helping you to gain a qualification, there are several other benefits.

- It gives you the opportunity to study an area of interest in detail and carry out your own research.
- It helps you to develop and demonstrate a variety of skills linked to project management, research, consultancy, analysis of data, communication and report writing.
- It gives you training in relating theory to practice.
- It challenges you to tackle a problem, situation or hypothesis with minimum supervision, in a creative yet sound way.

What does this guide cover?

Although no two reports will ever be exactly the same (or shouldn't be, anyway!), there are still a lot of hints and tips that can be given on the general process for completing a good report or dissertation (the terms 'dissertation' and 'report' will be used interchangeably throughout this guide). We'll provide guidelines on the researching and writing of such reports, drawing on the experiences of many people.

The focus will be on reports and dissertations required by undergraduate, diploma, or masters qualifications. This guide is not intended to cover coursework or pure doctoral theses. Nonetheless, it should be of interest to all students and practising managers who are required to carry out and write up research, whether this be for shorter assignments or for a workplace report.

We want this guide to be of practical help to you in completing your project so we have asked the advice of people who are writing dissertations at the moment or who have recently completed them, and sought the views of tutors on management courses. They have given us some *Top Tips* which we have included throughout the text.

TOP **TIP!**
Plan your time on both a daily and monthly basis and stick to self-imposed deadlines for stages of your work.

On a lighter note, we also give you some *Words of Wisdom* which should be taken tongue in cheek.

Words of **Wisdom!**
The sooner you fall behind, the more time you have to catch up.

Good luck with your project.

Ray Irving and *Cathy Smith*

What Makes an Outstanding Report or Dissertation?

There are many characteristics of a successful dissertation but here are 10 of the most important.

❶ The topic has been carefully chosen

The final report reflects how carefully you have selected your subject. It will show:

- how feasible the topic has been in terms of time and budget available
- how well you have been able to sustain it in terms of:
    - its breadth (was it too wide or too narrow?)
    - the opportunities to carry out research
    - its ability to interest and enthuse you
- whether several conclusions, and not just the one you anticipated, were equally valid
- how closely the objectives of all the stakeholders - the educational institution, your employer (where this is relevant), yourself and any other interested parties - have been met.

❷ *The dissertation should maintain the right balance between theory and practice*

The correct balance will vary according to the type of qualification.

- An undergraduate project will usually be based on theory but may be more practical if conducted as part of a work placement.
- A DMS will demand a strong, task-based approach.
- An MBA, MSc or MA dissertation may have a problem-solving element, often related to a real-life organisational situation, but also needs to make reference to appropriate theory and use models, concepts and other ideas.

❸ *The dissertation has clearly stated aims, scope and objectives*

These must remain in the foreground throughout the report. For example: the literature review should place your research work in context and the results of your research must be related back to the aims and objectives, indicating the extent to which they have been met.

❹ *The methodology is appropriate*

A good report demonstrates that appropriate research methods have been used in terms of the aims of the project, the time available and the associated costs.

❺ *The material featured in the final report has been carefully selected*

The report must keep to the point and is only concerned with the most important or relevant information. It does not contain all that you have discovered about the subject - quantity does not equal quality.

❻ *The report has a well balanced structure*

There should be a sensible split of material between the main text and the appendices and between chapters themselves. Its contents should look something like this:

- Title page
- Abstract or summary of about 200 words
- Acknowledgements
- Contents page
- Introduction, covering the purpose and aims of the study
- Literature review
- Methodology
- Investigations, results, analysis and discussion
- Summary and conclusions
- Recommendations
- References
- Appendices (supporting documents)

❼ *The dissertation is objective and analytical*

- There should be no evidence of bias or emotion.
- The emphasis should be on analysis, rather than on description.
- The conclusions must be valid in relation to the project and its results, neither too strong nor too weak.

❽ *It is highly readable*

This means that:

- it is understandable to all readers, even those who know little about the subject
- it avoids the use of jargon
- the spelling, grammar and punctuation used are correct and consistent
- research results and statistics are presented in an appropriate form, for example graphs, pie charts, histograms or tables.

❾ *It keeps to the required physical format*

This includes:

- the size of paper
- the size of margins
- spacing
- binding
- the overall length.

Find out how many copies are required, and in what medium. If paper copies are asked for, check whether originals are stipulated or whether photocopies will do. If on disk, what format should the files be in? Note: sometimes a mix of media is required.

⑩ *It is submitted on time*

Consult your supervisor at regular intervals, particularly at the beginning of the project when choosing a subject. Ensure that they have opportunities to comment on drafts as the report develops.

It is especially important to inform your supervisor if you have problems, particularly in case of sickness, bereavement or other exceptional circumstances and give notice in good time if you need an extension. Failure to consult on such matters will be regarded as discourteous and may affect your final grading. Similarly, resist the temptation to avoid your supervisor if you haven't made any progress. Talking to them may get you kick-started - discussion generates thoughts!

TOP **TIP!**

Outstanding projects have a 'spark', an indefinable something. This is evident where you have applied creative thought to a new, difficult or innovative area and produced something original.

Getting Started

Which **subject** will I choose?

How do I put together a **proposal**?

How am I going to get it done **on time**?

Choosing a Subject

The initial stage of writing a report or dissertation consists of identifying a suitable topic and then putting together a proposal. It can be the most difficult part of the exercise; it is certainly the most important. In some cases you will be given a topic to study or be asked to undertake a project that is directly related to your job. Even so, there is often room to choose a particular aspect of the subject and flexibility in the way you tackle it.

The following process is a good way of choosing a subject.

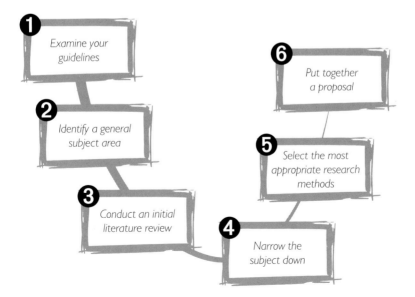

1. Examine your guidelines
2. Identify a general subject area
3. Conduct an initial literature review
4. Narrow the subject down
5. Select the most appropriate research methods
6. Put together a proposal

❶ *Examine your guidelines*

There are major differences between types of projects and dissertations for different qualifications. You need to find out, for example:

- what is the completion date - how much time have you got?
- the total number of words or pages needed - how long does it have to be ?
- the level of research needed - should it be practical, theoretical or both? Does it need to be original?

If anything is at all unclear, check with your tutor before you start to put your ideas together. It is crucial that you understand the guidelines.

❷ *Identify a general subject area*

Here are some ideas for finding a subject area:

- Look over assignments you have written in the past. Where have you received your best and worst marks?

- Track down previous reports and dissertations in your college or university library. Look at what others have done and at their recommendations for further research.

- Monitor the media for articles, speeches or comments which might indicate room for further research in particular fields.

- Think about your career. Do you want to specialise in one functional area of management, such as human resource management, or in one sector, such as public services or in a combination of both?

- If you are a member of a professional association, you should be able to attend local meetings and events. By talking to other managers you may be able to pick up an area of interest. These meetings are also an excellent way of finding managers and organisations who may be able to help you in your research.

- Is there a topic which you can derive from your work experience?

- Is there a new or emerging activity or development which you would like to pursue at work? Can you offer to work as an internal consultant on the project?

- Find out if any organisations have offered projects to your college with which they want help.

The Institute of Management's *'Management Thesaurus'* helps you to break the subject of management into six areas:

- Financial management
- Personnel management
- Operations management
- Marketing management
- Information management
- Management techniques

and gives you a detailed list of narrower terms in each area.

Once you have a rough idea of a topic ask yourself the following questions:

- *Does it interest me?* You may be spending up to a year on this project, at stages eating, drinking and sleeping with it. Are you quite confident that you won't be bored to tears with it after a couple of months? If you enjoy the subject, the research should be much easier. On the other hand, research will be extremely tedious if you have no interest in it.

- *How much do I know about the subject already?* It can be difficult starting completely from scratch. On the other hand, a fresh start can prove all the more rewarding.

- *Is it worth doing?* The project must add some value. This can be for a particular organisation or individual, or for the subject field in general. It should also be capable of several conclusions - all of equal validity. This means that if your research leads to a conclusion which is different from the one you anticipated, it will still be useful.

- *Is the subject well enough developed for me to write about it?* If the topic is very modern then there may have been little written about it. It can be very hard going in this case. On the other hand it may present a real opportunity and challenge to break new ground.

- *How difficult is it likely to be?* Remember which qualification you are taking. You don't need to write a PhD thesis for a diploma. Some subjects may rely on concepts and techniques which are too advanced for your level of study. You must be comfortable with what you are preparing to do.

• *What expertise is available?* You will need personal help throughout the project. Generally you will be matched up with a tutor for the period of your project but they may not be a specialist in that area. If you are going to work on an internal or external case study how much assistance can you expect to receive from the organisation concerned? How far will specialists in other organisations be able and willing to help you?

❸ Conduct an initial literature review

Chapter 4 provides details of how to do a literature search. At this stage you do not need to undertake an exhaustive study of the literature. You should be looking at the general subject, however, and trying to see which individual topics there are within it. This search will also give you a good idea of whether there is enough information on the subject for you to tackle the project effectively.

❹ Narrow the subject down

Ask yourself what you need to know about your topic. Try to clarify your aims and ,having done so, ask yourself questions on that topic that will need to be answered. Brainstorm ideas with fellow students or colleagues. You might like to draw a spider map or a Mind Map (the latter term is a Registered Trade Mark of Tony Buzan). This is where you start with a circle or square showing your central idea, attaching other narrower ideas to the centre as they come to you.

Example of a Spider Map

Self-catering

Camp   Hotel   Mobile

Caravan
                    Fixed

Barge /
Longboat

Europe
        USA   Cruise
Far East
        Africa

Cancel newspapers

Cancel milk   Abroad   Wales   Scotland
Care of animals   England
                    Mail   UK
Care of garden   Seaside
            Home   Inland

Security

Police   Take Granny
Insurers   THIS YEAR'S
            HOLIDAY
Neighbours   ARRANGEMENTS   Alternatives

Clothing requirements
                                Green Card
Luggage   Insurance arrangements
                                        Public transport
        Can cope with   Hire car
Allowed   Ferry
                    Take car
Currency   Ferry   Rail   Fly

            Passport
Visa

Don't forget general considerations such as:

- Could you apply the subject to a particular organisation? Would it be of value to that organisation?
- Is the topic too broad or too narrow? If you can't summarise the arguments for and against the topic in a few short sentences, then the topic is too broad.
- Does it still fit with your course aims? Have you gone off at a tangent?

You should be aiming to refine your subject so that it is sufficiently cohesive and focused.

Hypotheses

You may be required to develop hypotheses or you may wish to do so anyway to get your report started. A hypothesis is really an intelligent guess. You state this guess at the beginning of your project and then you go on to use research methodology to test whether the 'guess' or hypothesis is correct. It usually takes the form of relating two variables:

> *Hypothesis: By raising the price of Mont Plonk champagne,*
> *the number of sales decreases.*

You can begin with more than one hypothesis, but you should set a limit of no more than three or four.

❺ Select the most appropriate research methods

- Read through the chapters in this guide entitled *Doing the Research* and decide which method is the most suitable for your purpose. It may be, for example, that you are employed in a company that has undergone a major reorganisation and you want to use it as a case study.

- Be realistic. It is unlikely that you will be able to use every research method due to the limitations on your time and resources. It is best to choose one or two and to use them properly, in order to obtain reliable results.

- Find out what expertise is readily available before you choose a method. Do you know someone who is skilled in designing questionnaires? Is one of your lecturers expert at case studies?

TOP **TIP!**

Do not slavishly follow the data collection methods used by other students - they may not be relevant to you. Similarly, don't get caught up in complex research methods if simpler approaches will suffice.

❻ *Put together a proposal*

A written proposal is often asked for by a tutor because it allows them to judge whether you are attempting something that is relevant, focused and achievable. There are two main parts to a project proposal:

- what you are going to do
- how you are going to do it.

Your tutor will be able to give you advice not only on the subject, but on the research methods you aim to use. Remember, they will most probably have overseen many of these types of projects, so listen to their words of wisdom. They are generally extremely good at seeing when students have bitten off more than they can chew.

Once you have put the proposal together you can use the following checklist to make sure that you have included everything.

- *Why* - are you undertaking the research?
- *What* - are you hoping to find out or establish?
- *How* - are you going to find it out?
- *Where* - are you going to be doing your research?
- *When* - will you be doing the research?
- *Who* - are you going to turn to for advice and help?

TOP **TIP!**

Explain your proposal or hypothesis to a friend who knows nothing about your subject. If they don't understand it, you haven't formulated it clearly enough.

Planning the Project

The importance of developing and writing an action plan with detailed times and dates for each part of the project cannot be overstated. Although it takes time to do, you are actually saving time and worry in the long run. Ask any student why they had difficulties with their report or dissertation and they will most likely tell you that it was because they did not have a plan of action, had planned badly, or did not follow the plan they had originally devised.

Remember that the management report or dissertation usually runs concurrently with the other coursework you have to do. You may have a full-time job to cope with as well!

 Words of **Wisdom!**
By failing to prepare, you are preparing to fail.

The following step-by-step guide will help you formulate an action plan.

- Identify the different tasks involved.
- Time the tasks.
- Put a date to the tasks.

❶ *Identify the different tasks involved*

From your proposal you should have a clear idea of which general areas have to be completed. These could be:

- the literature search
- data collection
- analysis of the results
- writing it up.

Within each of these areas you should identify the individual tasks involved, for example:

The literature search

- Check library databases
- Search other electronic sources - CD-ROM, online, the Internet
- Gather documents (e.g. books, periodical articles)
- Conduct preliminary reading

Data collection (using a questionnaire as an example)

- Obtain sample - gather names and addresses
- Design and pilot questionnaire
- Send out questionnaire
- Input results

Analysis of the results

- Conduct statistical analyses
- Create graphs, pie-charts, etc.
- Draw up recommendations

Writing it up
- Devise layout and structure
- Write up:
  - the introduction
  - the literature review
  - a description of the methodology
  - the results, analysis and discussion
  - the summary, conclusions and recommendations
  - the abstract
- Compile references
- Proofread
- Organise the printing and binding.

A lot of these will run concurrently, for example while doing the literature search you could be gathering the names and addresses of those to be surveyed for data collection purposes. Some tasks you will need to do throughout the whole period of the project, such as continuing to read and search the literature. This will become easier as you get to know which sources to check and you will only be looking for material added since you last looked.

A robust model for the various stages of a report or dissertation is the **DIRECT** model.

- **D**escribe - your own or observed experience. What happens? What goes on? How do things work?
- **I**nvestigate - uncover more information or detail about the context of your study. This can be done by various means, such as interviews and questionnaires.
- **R**esearch - obtain primary or secondary data, identifying best practice, ideas, tools, techniques, models and frameworks. ➤

Information can come from desk research, the Internet, scanning databases, reading books and articles, or by obtaining primary data from the field.

- Evaluate/analyse - analyse the data obtained, making comparisons, judgements and inferences, to evaluate, explain or gain meaning from the data.
- Conclude - summarise, draw conclusions and frame action points from your analysis.
- Take stock - reflect on your own learning via this process. Identify personal development and action points.

❷ *Time the tasks*

You must now estimate the time needed to complete each task, although it is impossible to set exact time limits. Nevertheless, try to estimate how many hours each one will take - if you can. Always err on the side of caution by overestimating the time you will need. That way, if you fall behind you won't be too far adrift of your timetable.

Words of **Wisdom!**
Murphy's Law: Everything takes longer than you think.

❸ *Put a date to the tasks*

The key is to divide up the time you have available and set dates for the completion of specific tasks so that you can monitor your progress and adapt your working practices accordingly. Buy a diary just for the report or dissertation. If the project spans a year-end remember that you can buy diaries for academic years.

Start out with the submission date of your report or dissertation and then work backwards to discover when certain tasks have to be completed. Have a look at each task and the time it will take and then set up a calendar of events.

Get a copy of your course outline for the period of the project as this will provide you with dates for any assignments you have to hand in, and any placements and field trips. Identify any work and personal commitments, i.e. meetings, conferences, weddings, or holidays. These dates should be entered into your diary first. You can then plan around them. Don't be afraid of having holidays as long as you plan them in advance and work them into your schedule. A break can be a good thing. If there are things which you need to learn about to help you in your project, such as how to use a computer statistics package or a spreadsheet, book yourself time in advance to learn.

TOP **TIP!**

Book time on a computer if you haven't got your own, so you can undertake statistical analyses and type up the final report. Make arrangements as early as you can and then record these bookings in your diary. This will save you a lot of hassle later on, as there may be a queue of students wanting to use the wordprocessors near the submission date!

The next stage to enter in your diary is when you have to contact people or organisations, for example if you want to interview somebody, or if you want someone to test your questionnaire or proofread your final document.

Finally, allocate dates for completing each of the individual tasks you have identified. Convert the number of hours into weeks depending on how much time you estimate you will have to spend on the project each day.

TOP **TIP!**

Avoid working too many hours a day. It's counter-productive in the long run. Plan and regulate the hours you spend studying.

Disasters do happen. Ensure you have sufficient time for contingency plans, for example if the response rate to your questionnaire is very low and you need to follow up.

Here is an example of what one month of your project diary may look like (the one you use should have a lot more white space):

JANUARY

M	T	W	T	F	S	S
	1 Start designing questionnaire - ask Ruth if she'll look at it	**2**	**3** Contact Fly by Night Ltd to arrange interview	**4**	**5**	**6**
7	**8** Give Ruth questionnaire and print out address labels	**9**	**10**	**11**	**12** Cathy's wedding - all day	**13**
14	**15** Send out questionnaire	**16** Check latest edition of IMID CD-Rom	**17**	**18** HR project due in	**19**	**20**
21	**22**	**23** Conference Blackpool	**24** Conference Blackpool	**25**	**26**	**27**
28 Book computer for inputting questionnaire results	**29**	**30** Deadline for completion of questionnaires				

Words of **Wisdom!**
The only person to always get it done by Friday was Robinson Crusoe.

Remember that what you are doing here is setting yourself individual goals, which when accumulated will mean a completed project. These goals should follow the SMART acronym, in that they should be:

- **S**pecific - so that you have a clear idea of what you want to achieve.
- **M**easurable - establish criteria so that you can check that you are getting somewhere.
- **A**ttainable - challenging but achievable.
- **R**ealistic - practical and within current capability.
- **T**imetabled - because without dates to measure accomplishment you will lose track of where you are.

If you are working and are allowed study leave, you will need to identify peak times where a lot of work needs to be done. Book these study leave dates early.

TOP **TIP!**
Aim to complete your dissertation well before the deadline. Allow time for proofreading, finalising the bibliography and binding - and for things to go wrong!

27

Doing the
Research

4

Desk Research and the Literature Review

This stage in your project has several aims:

- to establish the parameters of your subject and the issues contained in it
- to identify sources of information on the topic
- to find out what has already been written on the subject so you can acknowledge this work and set yours in context
- to identify individuals and organisations who may be able to help with providing background information or case studies
- to finish with a list of references which relate directly back to your dissertation's aims and scope, and which demonstrate that you have read widely on the subject.

Undertaking Desk Research - A Checklist

❶ Review the amount of time you have available

Plan and organise your research accordingly, bearing in mind that you cannot read everything. This may be because:

- you do not have sufficient time
- some sources will be more relevant than others

• others cannot be tracked down or for some reason are unavailable
• there is substantial duplication in the field.

Make sure your research is as complete as possible without spending an inordinate amount of time scraping around for bits and pieces.

❷ *Take clear notes from the beginning*

Meticulous recording of references will help you to keep track of your research and will also save you time later when you come to write up references as part of your report. Your notes should record what is relevant to your research in your reading and your judgement of it. Everybody has their own way of keeping notes but it is a good idea to bear in mind these general points.

• Information on different topics should be stored separately - use ringbinders and dividers to separate topics. Number the pages so that you minimise the risk of mislaying vital information.
• Your notes should always record the details of the source of information - when you photocopy something make sure all the bibliographic details are on the photocopy and, if not, write them on (including the page numbers).
• Your notes should be flexible enough for you to add further information as it becomes available and to make deletions as items become less important or are duplicated elsewhere.
• You should appraise your notes regularly and reorganise them so they do not get out of hand.
• They should be neither so extensive nor so cryptic that you do not have a reasonable idea of what is in them at any given time.

TOP **TIP!**

Find out which reference or citation style you are required to use in your final report so you know which details you will need. It can be very time-consuming to backtrack and get this information later on.

❸ *Identify key concepts and phrases*

These introduce you to your chosen subject and can be used as search terms as your work proceeds. They can be revised and added to as your knowledge develops. This is where you should start referring to the types of information sources mentioned in the box below.

Examples of Types of Information Sources

- Management dictionaries and encyclopaedias
- Books
- Journals
- Newspapers
- Survey reports
- Market survey reports
- Annual reports
- Stockbroker and credit rating reports
- Government literature
- Conference/seminar proceedings
- Videos
- Maps
- Statistics
- World Wide Web sites
- Internet newsgroups and discussion lists
- Foreign language sources
- Grey literature (unpublished reports and papers)

❹ Find suitable libraries

Make the most of library services. Your first port of call should be your college library or the library of a professional management body, if you are a member (see Appendix 5 for a list of addresses). Another place to start is your public library. Although it may be too general for your needs, it may point you in the direction of other specialist libraries of which you may be unaware. If there is a subject specialist library, use it if you can, even if it means travelling. It will make research easier because you will find a wealth of relevant items collected together in one place.

When visiting a library, always check the catalogue before going to the shelves, otherwise you may miss some important sources. The books on your subject may not be grouped together in one place on the shelves and some may be out on loan. Don't be afraid to ask a librarian, especially a subject specialist, for help. They don't bite!

Databases available online, on CD-ROM and on the World Wide Web, are vital to your search and you must be prepared to pay for their use. Before travelling to libraries check on their access to these sources (see Appendices 2 and 3 on sources of information on management, markets and companies).

The libraries or databases that you use to carry out your research may hold the full text of relevant references. Bear in mind that libraries may charge you for such a service and that you may have to wait some time for obscure or popular items. Order these as early as you can in your research and make time to read the books thoroughly, and take notes, when they arrive. You may not be able to have the item for long and may not get hold of it again. Online services such as *UnCover* (see Appendix 2) can provide full-text articles very quickly but they can be expensive.

TOP **TIP!**

Photocopying articles can be very expensive and counterproductive. Sit down and read the article first, noting down points and quotations. Some articles which look promising may have very little in them and it can be a waste of time and money to copy them.

❺ Establish the objectives and parameters of your research

Try to obtain a ready-made reading list or, if such a list is not available, compile your own. Such a list should contain a selection of basic texts on the subject, including both new and classic books, and recent journal articles. It should lead you to the major theorists as well as suggesting sources of examples of practical applications and case studies. In this way you will be able to:

- define your subject
- find out what is the state of the art
- discover how common is the theory, technique or problem
- uncover the related topics
- establish which are the leading or significant companies in the field
- identify the major authors (the proponents and the critics)
- learn about the traditional and the emerging models
- pinpoint gaps in the collective knowledge.

You can also begin to refine the parameters of your project in terms of factors such as time periods, geographic spread and choice of materials.

It is important to keep an open mind as you carry out research, as some aspects of your subject may become more important than others and new ones may open up.

35

TOP **TIP!**

Keep a notebook where you can write down flashes of inspiration regarding the project or dissertation, for later use.

---

❻ *Follow up your initial research*

When you have got to grips with the basics of the subject, you will need to carry out a more detailed literature search. Follow up footnotes and references in the sources you already have and re-visit some of the libraries and databases to undertake more in-depth work on certain aspects of your subject.

At this stage you may need to contact specialist organisations. Be aware that people there will assume that you have a basic understanding of the subject. Remember that in many cases these organisations are under no obligation to help you. Be patient and accept that the first source you try may not be able to help and may refer you to others.

❼ *Evaluate sources*

Use your various sources to:
- give you an overview of, or introduction to, a subject
- establish the key authors in the area
- provide you with a piece of specific information, or clarification of a particular point
- establish if there is anything new or different that you haven't come across before
- acquire an in-depth understanding, following a reasoned argument
- give you background information on a related topic to which you may wish to refer.

TOP **TIP!**

Identify the core journals for your chosen subject and scan each new issue throughout the length of your project.

You will most probably use secondary sources such as books and journal articles in your desk research but primary sources are sometimes essential. For example, consider whether a piece of legislation or a particular report is significant for your subject. Ensure you have read the original legislation or report. Don't rely solely on the summaries and interpretations offered by secondary sources.

Evaluate carefully the sources you use; it is important not to take any source at face value. All writers work from a particular point of view. It is inevitable that even those who purport to be independent will have a certain bias. Consider the writer's background, target audience and objectives in writing. Evaluate the writer's conclusions in the light of your existing knowledge of the subject.

TOP **TIP!**

Keep records of all the documents you have looked at, even if you're not sure you will use them. A card index or sticky notes are useful. Tracking down where you originally saw something can be an infuriating waste of time. It didn't seem relevant when you first saw it, but now ...

❺

Questionnaires and Sampling

What is a questionnaire?

A questionnaire is a method of obtaining specific information from a particular group of people about a defined problem so that the data, after analysis and interpretation, give you a better appreciation of the situation in question. Questionnaires may be administered in several different ways: by personal or telephone interview, or sent by post, fax or e-mail.

Questionnaires can take one of two approaches: *structured* (consisting of questions with pre-coded answers) or *unstructured* (where the respondent can phrase his/her own answer). A combination of the two approaches is the most popular method. Remember that structured questionnaires can provide data that is easy to analyse, because responses are most often of the yes / no / don't know type. Unstructured questionnaires are more difficult to analyse as respondents can choose their own answer and phraseology, but they have the advantage that they do not place any restrictions on an individual's answers.

Designing A Questionnaire - A Checklist

The questionnaire is a vital part of many student surveys and there is no easy way to design a series of questions: it remains largely a matter of art rather than science. This is one suggested method.

❶ *Relate your questionnaire to your research objectives*

The objectives you set in your proposal provide the framework for the contents of the questionnaire. Clarify what you want to achieve. Distinguish that which is essential from that which is nice to know.

❷ *Select the most appropriate method to administer the questionnaire*

This depends on the subject of the survey, the nature of the survey population and the resources (time and money) available. The traditional methods for obtaining responses to questionnaires are personal interview (like the market research surveys you may have taken part in on the high street), telephone or post. Each of these methods has advantages and disadvantages. New methods of administering questionnaires include fax and e-mail which combine both the benefits and the problems of telephone and postal questionnaires.

In general, postal questionnaires are better for factual data and obtaining basic information on attitudes. They are also more appropriate for very large or geographically scattered samples. Face-to-face (and to a lesser extent telephone) ones are better for more complex information. If you're sending out postal questionnaires within an organisation you may be allowed to use the internal mail system and so cut down on costs. If you are posting questionnaires to a wider area, consider enclosing a stamped addressed envelope, or at least an addressed envelope, to obtain a better response.

The following table highlights the key features of each traditional method of administering questionnaires:

	Face-to-face	Telephone	Postal
Acceptability	reasonable	doubtful	open choice
Recruitment	controlled	controlled	self-selecting
Response rate	fixed	fixed	variable
Reaching scattered sample	moderate	fast	slow
Speed	poor	very good	very good
Interaction / rapport	very good	good	poor
Complexity of interview	possible	limited	impossible
Interviewer bias	present	present	absent
Interview length	up to 1 hour (pre-arranged)	10-15 mins	30 questions (maximum)
Resources needed	large	substantial	moderate

❸ *Obtain permission to administer the questionnaire*

At the very least you must inform your tutor what you are going to do. This is because you will be trading on the good name of the college in carrying out your research. If any other organisation is involved make sure you get the appropriate permission. Apart from smoothing your path, it may lead to suggestions for improvements and offers of help.

❹ *Work out what you are going to do with the results*

Even a low response rate may well give you lots of paper to sort and sift, or plenty of data to key into a PC analysis package, spreadsheet or database. Irrespective of whether the analysis will be done manually or electronically, think in advance of the ease or difficulty of data management and the facilities available to analyse the responses.

On the other hand, don't focus so much on ease of analysis that it impacts on ease of use for the respondent or relevance of the exercise. Working out how you will use the responses will also help determine the mix of structured and unstructured questions, and whether all questions will apply to all respondents.

❺ *Plan the question sequence*

It is good practice, whichever method is used, to:
- start with one or two general questions which are easy to answer
- explore present behaviour, i.e. what is being used / done now, before asking about the past or future
- follow a logical order so that the respondent is not confused
- position sensitive questions towards the middle or the end
- ensure that ideas, which may influence answers to later questions, are not put into the respondent's head at an earlier stage
- leave 'classification' answers to the end (e.g. 'Which age range do you fall into?').

❻ *Design precise questions*

You should by now have determined the topics to be covered and what level of detail is needed. The next stage is to consider the following:

- **Open or closed?** Questions can be closed (as in structured questionnaires) or open-ended (unstructured questionnaires). The anticipated answers to a closed question are pre-coded with simple instructions to the interviewer or respondent, for example, 'Circle number' or 'Please tick ONE box only' or 'Please tick as applicable'. Allow for 'Don't know' or 'Not stated'. It is advisable to pre-code as many questions as possible - open-ended questions may provide richer data in that the respondent answers in his or her own words, but the answers have to be put into coding categories afterwards anyway.

- **Confusion and understanding.** Avoid long or technical words and jargon. Watch out for possible ambiguity or any lack of clarity. Words such as 'frequently', 'often', 'regularly' or 'usually' need to be qualified. Avoid double negatives - 'Would you not drink a non-alcoholic beer?'. Ask about a single issue only - avoid questions such as 'What do you think of the economic policies of this Government and how do you think they should be modified, if at all?'

- **Attitude questions.** The simplest approach is to put a statement to the respondent with which they can agree or disagree. For example:

	1 Agree	2 Disagree	3 Neither agree nor disagree	4 Don't know
There is a sensible balance between my work and my personal life	☐	☐	☐	☐

This lacks sensitivity, however, as you have no idea how strongly those who reply 'agree' do agree, nor how strongly people disagree. In order to get an indication of the strength or weakness with which an attitude is held, you need to construct rating scales. Two commonly used types of rating scales are known as *Likert* and *Semantic differential*.

Likert: a statement is put to the respondent who is asked, 'Please tell me how much you agree or disagree with these statements', e.g.:

	1 Strongly agree	2 Slightly agree	3 Neither agree nor disagree	4 Slightly disagree	5 Strongly disagree
I have good opportunities *for career development…*	☐	☐	☐	☐	☐

The responses are analysed by allocating weights to scale positions. You might allocate 5 to 'strongly agree', 3 for mid-point, 1 point for strongly disagree or vice-versa - but be consistent. If the scale battery includes both positive and negative attitude statements, then 'strongly agree' for a negative statement rates 1, not 5.

Semantic differential: These are easier to administer and more meaningful when rating responses about the specific attributes of named products and services. For example, if the product is a motor car, you might construct the following double-ended scales:

	Good					Poor
Acceleration:	☐	☐	☐	☐	☐	

It is also common to use points, e.g.:

	Good	1	2	3	4	5	Poor
Reliability		☐	☐	☐	☐	☐	

Semantic scales can be either mono-polar (for example, bitter - not bitter; modern - not modern) or bi-polar (for example, modern - old fashioned; strong - weak).

❼ Think of design and page lay-out

Don't cramp the respondent or the interviewer - leave room for the answers! Instructions should be completed in a different typestyle (such as bold print, underlined, upper case or in brackets). An attractive layout is all the more important in a postal questionnaire, as it has a significant effect on the response rate.

In a postal questionnaire, give the respondent the option of filling in their name, but assure them that their answers will remain confidential. It will help you to identify non-respondents. Leave space for respondents to confirm whether they are willing to be interviewed for further information if appropriate.

Check that clear instructions are given on how to return the questionnaire, to whom and the deadline date.

❽ Pilot the questionnaire

Ask colleagues and friends to try out the questionnaire. The piloting will identify whether it is too long or too short, bearing in mind both the convenience of the respondents and your data collection needs. It will also help you to spot and clarify any ambiguous questions and any problems with layout or ordering, for example.

❾ *Prepare for responses*

Don't be surprised by a low response rate for postal questionnaires. 5-10% is quite usual and respectable. You may even achieve 30% if you have a motivated survey group. If you feel that the response is too low, however, you can send out reminder letters after a couple of weeks. For face-to-face or telephone interviews, you may well receive 5 or more refusals before you get an agreement to take part.

*TOP **TIP!***

Improve the response rate to your questionnaire by:

- *enclosing a stamped addressed envelope*
- *making your questionnaire short, to the point and easy to complete*
- *including the return address in case the envelope is lost*
- *providing a contact number in case of a query*
- *promising to give respondents feedback on the survey results.*

If you need further details the following may be useful:

- **Using questionnaires and surveys to boost your business**
  Nick Evans and Institute of Management Foundation
  London   Pitman   1995
  (Better business performance series)
  ISBN: 027361181X   £15.99

- **Questionnaire design, interviewing and attitude measurement**
  2nd edition
  A N Oppenheim
  London   Pinter   1992
  ISBN: 1855670445   £15.99

- **Questionnaire design**
  Paul Hague
  London   Kogan Page   1993
  (The Kogan Page market research series)
  ISBN: 0749409177   £12.95

- **Questionnaires: design and use**
  2nd edition
  Doug R Berdie, John F Anderson and Marsha A Niebuhr
  Metuchen, NJ   Scarecrow Press   1986
  ISBN: 0810818841   £22.50

Sampling

This is only a basic introduction to the most important points of sampling. Double check with one of your tutors or ask a colleague with statistical knowledge to ascertain whether your proposed sample is valid.

In this section we look at two of the most common sampling methods: *random sampling* and *quota sampling*. Whatever sampling method is used, however, the object is to select individuals in such a way that the sample is representative of the population being surveyed. A population need not be composed of people, but can consist of, for example, industries, organisations, or retail outlets. In determining sample size, it is common practice to ensure that there are at least 50, and preferably 100, items representing even the smallest group likely to be considered.

Random sampling

Random samples are appropriate for a general population where you wish to minimise the margin of error in the results. Random does not mean haphazard - it refers to a definite method of selection in which each item in the population has an equal chance of being chosen. To meet these requirements, it is necessary to locate every individual in the survey population on a list which is complete and up to date.

An example of random sampling is as follows. Assume 500 individuals need to be drawn from a population of 5,000 - the sample will amount to 1/10. A table of random numbers or a computer program can be used to draw the first at random, for example, individual number 3, and to generate the names of the other individuals, for example, numbered 13, 23, 33 and so on, until the sample has been filled; i.e. to add 10 four hundred and ninety-nine times.

Random samples are inappropriate when investigating populations:

- where some individuals are difficult to get hold of, for example managers in large companies who may be 'protected' by a secretary
- which include individuals or organisations critical to the survey
- which are composed of organisations of unequal sizes
- on which you have inadequate information - random selection from an incomplete list could result in the omission of key respondents.

Quota sampling

Quota samples are commonly used in both consumer and industrial market research. In this method, selection of sample members is non-random and is designed to mirror relevant characteristics in the population. In consumer markets the most common strata for sampling are sex, age and income/social class. In industrial surveys the most common strata are industry type and organisation size.

In a *proportionate* sample equal proportions are sampled from each stratum and it is assumed the variation within individual groups is relatively equal. In a *disproportionate* sample you will oversample small-sized strata at the expense of large-sized strata, but restore their due weights in the population when the total results are being considered.

A quota sample takes account of the wealth of published statistical data. A good deal is known about the structure of populations in developed countries (whether consumer, trade or industrial) and these records are regularly updated. Governments collect and publish statistics, as do professional, industrial and trade associations.

Further details about sampling will be found in the following.

- **A handbook of market research techniques**
  Robin Birn, Paul Hague and Phyllis Vangelder (eds)
  London   Kogan Page   1990
  ISBN: 0749402008   £45.00

- **Marketing research**
  5th edition
  Peter Chisnall
  London   McGraw-Hill   1996
  ISBN: 0077091752   £21.95

- **The marketing research process**
  4th edition
  Margaret Crimp and Len Tiu Wright
  Englewood Cliffs, NJ   Prentice Hall   1995
  ISBN: 0132028395   £21.95

TOP **TIP!**

Make detailed notes of how you chose your sample, as you will need to include these details in the final report.

❻

Interviews and Observation

Interviews

Interviews can be used:

- to gather background information before sending out a questionnaire
- as a follow-up to a questionnaire to gather further detailed information
- as part of a case study
- on their own as the total research method.

Carrying Out An Effective Interview - A Checklist

❶ Select the individuals to be interviewed

The method of selection will depend on why you are using interviews. If you are following up a questionnaire, potential interviewees can be obtained either from your sample or from those who have volunteered to provide further information. If you are pursuing a case study you will want to talk to those involved in the situation or problem you are studying. Otherwise the need to contact certain people for interview will be predetermined by your proposal, for example personnel officers in medium-sized organisations in a particular locality. Keep notes for your final report on how the interviewees were chosen.

❷ *Do your homework and allow the interviewees to do theirs*

Make sure you have read up not only on the topic of the interview but have also gained some background information on the interviewee and on their organisation. Remember, he or she will be a busy person who won't want their time wasted by someone who is unsure of their brief. For this reason conduct your interviews well into your project at a time when you feel comfortable with your topic of investigation. Give interviewees a good idea of what you will be interviewing them about in advance, thus enabling them to get some background material together. Make sure you know where to find the interviewee's organisation: you don't want to get there late.

❸ *Plan the interview*

Like a questionnaire (see Chapter 5), the interview can be structured or unstructured, with the same advantages and disadvantages applying. Even if the interview is unstructured you should at least prepare some questions to ask, no matter how general. Think why you are asking each question. Is it relevant to your research? Prepare a form for each interview where you can enter the name and organisation of the interviewee and to which you can attach any supplementary sheets of notes or material they provide. This way you can keep everything together and avoid getting items confused with other interviews you may be doing.

❹ *Conduct the interview*

Start off by restating the purpose of the interview and asking the interviewee if you can tape record the interview (if they say yes, make sure the tape recorder is running!). Pose a few general questions to put the interviewee at ease but most importantly, let them do the talking and avoid putting words into their mouth. Always keep in mind why you are doing the interview and what the subject is. This way you can bring the interview back on course if it wanders, but be prepared for a few surprises. Don't filter out information which you may think irrelevant: new avenues could open up for you.

Don't attempt to write down the interview word-for-word, but do make brief notes of important points.

Words of Wisdom!

The most common source of mistakes in management decisions is the emphasis on finding the right answers rather than on asking the right questions.

❺ *Write it up*

Replay any tape recording as soon as possible after the interview and make detailed notes. Your notes may be difficult to decipher a few weeks later.

❻ *Learn from each interview*

Like most things, you will get better as you do more interviews. Identify which were the best ways of asking questions, but try to achieve consistency between interviews.

❼ *Write to thank each interviewee*

Write to thank them for their time, briefly acknowledging the value of their contribution. If possible, you should later send them a copy of your final report or dissertation. If you are dealing with a large group of people a summary will suffice.

TOP **TIP!**

Practise your interviewing skills on a colleague or friend first.

Observation

Observation is another widely used research methodology as it can be more reliable to see what people do than depend on what they say they do. It may not be a feasible solution for you, however, as it is very time-consuming.

In order to make the data as valid as possible you need to observe people's behaviour over a long period of time. This is because people can act differently:

- when they know they are being observed, changing their behaviour, and thus skewing the results. It has been found that behaviour reverts to normal after the people being observed get used to the idea, however.

- at different times, depending on factors such as their mood or the issue being discussed.

There is also a danger of bias on the part of the researcher, particularly when members of the group are known to you. To minimise this problem you can adopt a structured approach where you have decided what you want to observe, how you are going to record events and how often. You can make use of existing schedules, charts and grids or you can devise your own.

Unless you are observing groups of people in public places, such as a railway station, always let people know why you are observing them and in what way, and obtain their permission first. Reassure them that you will preserve their anonymity.

TOP **TIP!**

Keep an open mind. Don't just see what you want to see or hear what you want to hear.

Case Studies

There is a good chance that your dissertation will centre on a case study of a particular organisation or feature one or more smaller case studies. A case study in this context is not the same as those used for teaching. It involves writing up a specific investigation which you have undertaken with individuals and organisations. It will encompass other research techniques, such as desk research, questionnaires, interviews and observation.

The first stage in undertaking a case study is to identify what you are looking at and why. Examples of case study topics are:

- an industrial dispute
- the merging of two organisations
- the career development of individuals
- the impact of new legislation.

Case studies can either look at something that has happened (for example a merger) or something that is happening (for example the implementation of a computer system). If you are planning to do a case study of an event which is happening or will happen, consider whether you will be able to see it through within your own timetable. It may not finish until after the report deadline or you may not be able to attend important meetings because you are otherwise engaged.

Words of **Wisdom!**

If you are attempting the impossible, you will fail. Keep it realistic.

It is much easier to conduct a case study if you identify points to look for before you begin. For example:

- what led up to the event?
- what happened during the event?
- what action was taken and what were the effects?
- what was the conclusion?
- what has taken place since?

Your literature review of this or similar events should help you to identify particular areas of interest to investigate.

Make sure that your remit is defined in other practical ways. Agree factors with the organisation such as:

- the amount of time available to you
- the facilities available to you
- the people to whom you will be allowed access.

It is important that all staff concerned are told what you are doing and why in order to allay any suspicions and to create a climate of trust. Although you want to be accepted by staff you still need to remain distant enough to be objective.

TOP **TIP!**

Deal sensitively and confidentially with any personal grievances or problems you may encounter in the course of carrying out your case study.

Bringing it all Together

How can I *analyse* my **data**?

What is the best **graph** or **chart** to use?

How should I **structure** my report?

Analysing your Results

This section looks at analysing the results of both quantitative and qualitative research. Remember, you're doing a course in management, not mathematics. You don't have to be a statistical genius to analyse your results.

Analysing Your Results - A Checklist

❶ *Decide how to store the data*

Even before you have received all your survey results back, you should have organised a way of storing and analysing them. This can be done by hand. You may need to design some kind of form to collate or summarise the data. It is much better, however, if you can use a computer software package, especially if you want to produce graphs and charts. In most cases a spreadsheet package will suffice. Don't be put off by this though; most modern software is inherently easy to use, with plenty of help available. The only difficulty you may come across is if you are attempting a complex statistical analysis, and the problems here will most probably be caused by your understanding of the statistics rather than the software.

Set up your spreadsheet so that you can start entering data as soon as you receive them.

It may look something like this.

	A	B	C	D	E	F	G
1	Name	Organisation	Sex	Age	Organisation Size	Salary	No. of previous jobs
2	Joe Bloggs	Fly by Night Ltd	M	35	Small	10000	6
3	Jane Owen	C U Later Co	F	40	Medium	15000	2
4	John Boddy	J I T Solutions	M	27	Large	9000	1
5	Bob Smith	Fly by Night Ltd	M	51	Small	19500	3
6							
7							

Each row represents an individual and each column an item of research.

Note that a spreadsheet can be used to store numbers (quantitative data) and words or phrases (qualitative data). Pure qualitative data though will generally need to be analysed by hand.

❷ *Sort the data*

Once you have entered the data you can sort them into different sections, such as:

- personal details - variables, such as the age or sex of participants
- work details - the size of the organisations, the participants' salary etc.
- subject details - the different areas covered by the questionnaire, interview, observation exercise etc.

❸ *Clarify what you are looking for*

Check what you set out to do in your proposal. It will indicate the areas of prime interest; for example where you are looking at gender difference, it is important to sort the information according to the sex of the participants.

❹ *Calculate the statistics and compile other results*

Structured data

Statistical or arithmetical processes can be applied to describe structured data. These include: percentages or proportions; averages or measures of central location; standard deviation or other measures to describe the dispersion. These simple statistics are easy to calculate and represent most of what people need to know for many data sets. Don't overcomplicate things - the vast majority of real applications need only the most basic of statistical techniques.

If you are considering using more sophisticated techniques make sure you understand how to use them properly.

Words of **Wisdom!**

Numbers are like people; torture them enough and they'll tell you anything.

Unstructured data

With unstructured data you should:

- tabulate results. Identify common groupings. For example: "4 out of 5 interviewees felt unhappy with their career development opportunities."
- generalise. Note any overriding thoughts. For example: "there was a general feeling that more could be done within each organisation to improve the flow of information."
- write out any specific points. For example: "One interviewee said: 'I would like to see internal job advertisements sent to each member of staff rather than put on the main noticeboard'."

63

❺ *Illustrate the data*

To make it easier for you to spot any trends in your results it is useful to put the data into graphs, charts or tables. There are many cases though when you can simply write out the results, for example:

- Out of 50 questionnaires sent out, 20 were returned, giving a 40% response rate.

The most important graphs or charts can be put straight into your final report. There are several types available.

Pie charts

Pie charts are good at showing how a total is broken down into its component parts, but they make it difficult to compare exact values.

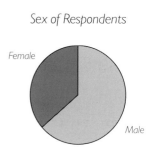

Sex of Respondents

Female

Male

Bar charts

In a bar chart, the bar itself represents the value of the factor being measured. It is therefore important to have a scale, remembering that the base line should be zero or else the data can look misleading. The label at the bottom of the bar does not have to represent the factor being measured - it may represent a period of time, for example. In such a case, more than one bar can be drawn, against one label, enabling different factors to be compared.

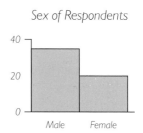

Sex of Respondents

Male *Female*

Histograms

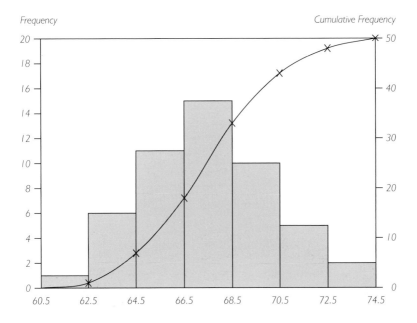

Histograms are often confused with bar charts, but there is one major difference. In a histogram the width of the bar, not just the height, is used to signify the size of the range. They are useful in illustrating a frequency distribution. A cumulative frequency curve can be added.

Other charts which can be used include:

- *cumulative frequency curves* - especially useful for pareto analysis, which identifies 20% of the variables responsible for 80% of the variation

- *gantt charts* - actual performance is mapped against planned performance on a time scale

- *pictograms* - a picture or icon is used to represent the data

- *straight line graphs* - two quantities which have a linear relationship are plotted against each other on a graph, with the result being a straight line

- *scatter diagrams* - a graph plotting values of two variables to illustrate the relationship between them.

- *time series* - a quantity of a factor is graphed against a time scale.

Only use colour in your graphs and charts if you know how to use it well - otherwise it can be confusing. If you do use it remember that you will need a colour printer for the final report.

If you need further details the following are useful introductions:

- **Understanding statistics in a week**
  Gareth Lewis and Institute of Management Foundation
  London   Hodder and Stoughton   1996
  (IM business in a week series)
  ISBN: 0340655046   £5.99

- **Basic business statistics: concepts and applications**
  5th edition
  Mark L Berenson and David M Levine
  Englewood Cliffs, NJ   Prentice Hall International   1992
  ISBN: 1306578080   £20.95

- **Statistics for management**
  5th edition
  Richard I Lewin and David S Rubin
  Englewood Cliffs, NJ   Prentice Hall International   1991
  ISBN: 0138472033

*TOP **TIP!***

A picture can paint a thousand words because it is used to represent something as simply and as clearly as possible. Choose the most appropriate picture.

9

Writing it up

This chapter contains advice on structuring your report or dissertation and on what should be included in each section. There are also some general guidelines on good writing practice and on the final presentation.

TOP **TIP!**

Don't leave writing up until the end - writing up as you go along provokes ideas and can help structure thoughts.

The structure of a dissertation or report

What follows is the layout of a typical, standard report. This is to help writers of reports to organise their material and arguments coherently and to help readers to find their way around. It is important, however, to check on the format which your college or organisation expects.

Title page

This includes the title (which should be short, precise and informative), your name and the date. It may also include the name of your college or university and department as well as the name of your company (where the latter is relevant to this piece of work).

Reconsider the title when you have finished writing up your dissertation to ensure that it still accurately reflects your work.

Abstract or (executive) summary

This is a description, in about 200 words, of the objectives of your study, which methods you used in your investigations and what conclusions were reached. This helps the readers decide if it is worth spending time reading the report and also provides some landmarks to orientate readers as they move through the report. If a copy of your final document is to be added to the college library you may be required to add some keywords to your abstract. This will help the library index your dissertation when the time comes.

Acknowledgements

Use this section to attribute any professional assistance and support you have had.

Contents page

Ensure that the section headings and page numbers referred to in the list of contents match up with the actual headings and page numbers in the rest of the document. Include a table of figures.

Introduction

Explain the purpose of the study (what led you to do this research), the aims and any hypotheses, and the scope of the project, including any limitations. Refer to relevant background information which puts your work in context. Outline what is to be found in the rest of the report.

TOP **TIP!**
A glossary of terms can prove invaluable.

Literature review

The purpose of the literature review is to set your work in context against the background of previous work. The amount of literature considered will depend on the amount which has already been written on your chosen subject. It should be selective, however, and deal only with the most relevant sources you have found. Follow a logical progression by moving from general to more specific material, from theory to practice and from historical to up-to-date information. Finish by referring to your own work.

Methodology

This is where you record how you investigated the problem and why particular techniques were used and others were rejected. Show how you have used appropriate theories or models and discuss their advantages and disadvantages. Describe the range of your research, for example the size of the sample used for a questionnaire.

Results, analysis and discussion

- Restate your aims and hypotheses and discuss how closely your aims were met and hypotheses proved.

- Examine the methodology to judge if there were any shortcomings and suggest ways it might have been improved.

- Interpret the results of your research to demonstrate their significance. Show how they add to the existing body of knowledge on the subject by comparing them with the findings of other research studies that you have come across in your literature survey.

71

• Explain any unexpected results. Where your results differ from those of previous research you need to give possible reasons. Where things went wrong, say so, but provide suggestions for improvements. If the lecturer can see you have learned from the experience you will gain, not lose, marks.

• Clearly number and title any graphs, tables or other graphics and introduce them within the text. If the graphic illustrates a key point it should be placed as close to that point as possible.

Summary and conclusions

This is an important section because some readers will read only the summary, the introduction and the conclusions. It is essential that the conclusions are related to the research question, drawn from the results and are not produced out of context. Don't try to make more of your results than your evidence suggests. They should be a suitable platform for the recommendations. If you think there should be further research undertaken in any particular area then point this out, making clear where you think your own research is limited and what could be done to improve the results.

Words of **Wisdom!**
A conclusion is simply the place where you got tired of thinking.

Recommendations

Recommendations should follow the conclusions and be as clear as possible, giving precise actions. Recommendations should be :
1. numbered
2. realistic
3. prioritised.

Allocate responsibility for their implementation to a particular person or group and indicate a timetable for their implementation. Suggest targets, measurement criteria, resource implications and any likely difficulties. Try to put yourself in the shoes of those to whom you are making the recommendations.

TOP **TIP!**

Try to get the recommendations commented upon by any organisations which have been involved in your research; this adds to the quality of the report.

References

See Appendix 1 for advice on citations.

Appendices

These are supporting documents which would obstruct the flow of the main report. They offer optional reading which does not bear directly on the main themes and conclusions. For example, if you have circulated a questionnaire in the course of your research, include a blank copy of the form. Appendices should be introduced and referred to in an appropriate place in the main text. Think whether it is easy to find each appendix. An assessor will not want to have to hunt around to find it.

Writing your report or dissertation

Treat each section separately; do not try to write the piece as one document. Write your chapters in order, however, as this will ensure that they follow on more logically. In the introduction to each chapter refer back to the previous one and link them together. Although you should write the introduction first, review and revise it at the end to take account of any changes which have taken place during the writing of the rest of the report.

Here are some rules to help you when writing up the report.

• Strive for clarity to avoid misunderstandings.

• Be analytical, not descriptive.

• Use logical arguments.

• Avoid assertions - opinions and conclusions must be supported by evidence.

• Keep your message straightforward without oversimplifying it.

• Write positively, as negative statements can be difficult to understand. For example, instead of "It is not unnecessary to change the system" use "It is necessary to change the system".

• Use the active voice as it is easier to understand than the passive. For example, instead of "The new computer system was criticised by employees" use "The employees criticised the new computer system".

- Take an objective stance rather than a subjective one. For example, instead of "Carpeting not only looks attractive but is easier to maintain than a hardwood floor" use "Carpeting not only looks attractive but according to the Head of Facilities Management is easier to maintain than a hardwood floor".

- Do not use emotive language. For example, instead of "The company has a successful recruitment programme but its turnover rate is shocking" use "The company has a successful recruitment programme but its turnover rate is very high".

- Avoid long and complex sentences, especially those with several subordinate clauses.

- Use long words only when they are appropriate; choose short words and phrases for conciseness and clarity.

- Avoid the use of sexist or ageist language. For example, use "staffing" not "manning".

- Employ technical terms and acronyms only when they are unavoidable or where you are sure your audience will understand them. A glossary may be required. On the other hand avoid colloquial language.

- Do not copy the work of other students or authors without due acknowledgement. Your college will take an extremely serious view of plagiarism. Make sure that if you wish to use sentences from other works you include them in quotation marks and always acknowledge their source. If you paraphrase other writers' ideas these must also be fully acknowledged. See Appendix 1 on references and citations.

TOP **TIP!**

Save your work daily to a back-up disk because accidents do happen. Take great care of your disks and keep them in separate places. Label them clearly. Print out your work regularly as well so if something does go wrong at least you have a hard copy.

Presentation and submission

Spelling and grammar

It should go without saying that your use of spelling, grammar and punctuation should be correct and consistent. Don't forget to use the spell checker on your PC but don't use this as a substitute for reading the finished document through carefully. Spell checkers do not trap all errors and can even create them. If you are not very good at spotting mistakes find someone who is.

You need access to a good dictionary, for example *Chambers English Dictionary* or the *Concise* or *Compact Oxford English Dictionary*. Similarly a thesaurus is a useful source for finding alternative terms: the best known is *Roget's Thesaurus of English Words and Phrases*.

If you need a reference book on punctuation the following may help:

- **You have a point there**
  Eric Partridge
  London Routledge 1990
  ISBN: 0415050758 £9.99

Layout

Layout and style are very important, so make full use of word processing techniques. Make the report easier to read by using devices such as **bold**, *italics*, or <u>underlining</u> for headings and subheadings. Use different font sizes and indentations where appropriate. Make sure you don't overdo them, however, and use them consistently. For long dissertations you may need to use a running header (usually the number and title of the chapter).

Review

Review what you have written. This is best done after an interval when the ideas are still new but you are fresher to analyse critically what you have written and can view it with more perspective. You will often find more effective ways of expression or errors you missed originally. Check the dissertation's content, structure and readability. Ask someone else to read through it for you.

One way of checking how readable your writing is, is to use a 'readability index calculator'. There are a number of different types of these, but one of the most common is the *Fog Index*. It is calculated by adding the average number of words in a sentence to the percentage of long words (generally speaking, words which have more than two syllables), and then multiplying the figure by 0.4. For example:

average sentence length + percentage of long words = ? x 0.4 =

$$24 + 11 = 35 \times 0.4 = 14$$

The final figure is supposed to be equivalent to the number of years of full-time education a reader would need to understand your writing easily and efficiently. Remember, it's not 100% accurate, but it will give you a good idea.

77

Presentation

- It is common for colleges to request a report which is typed on one side of the paper only. One and a half or double spacing is also normally required to make the dissertation easier to read and mark.

- If you use a numbering or lettering system for your sections and subsections, don't make it too complicated. Its purpose is to give a clear indication of the structure of the report or to make reference to particular points easier. The most common method in use is the decimal system:

  1.
      1.1
      1.2
          1.2.1 etc.

- Ensure that you do not exceed the permitted length as you will probably be penalised for doing so.

- Find out the requirements for binding well in advance and check on the cost and the time it will take. Make sure you are happy with the final report before it goes to the binders - particularly that the pages are in the correct order.

TOP **TIP!**
If your dissertation is to be bound, allow a slightly larger left hand margin so that even if the book doesn't open fully when bound, the text can still be easily read.

And Finally ...

Here is some parting advice from those who have learned the hard way!

Begin in good time - it will take you 100% more time than you think it will, so start 50% earlier than you think you need to.

Plan your work schedule before you start. Decide what needs to be done and write a timetable. It may have to be adjusted slightly as you go, but sticking to it will give you control over your work and confidence that you can finish on time.

Come up with a working title or key sentence of what your dissertation is all about. Blow it up in a large, bold font and hang it up where you can glance at it regularly.

Start off with the research. Then work from your results and findings.

Make sure the information you collect is usable - identify what you want to collect and decide what you are going to do with it before you start collecting.

Keep in touch with all the personal contacts you make in the course of your research. Let them know what you have achieved. This is not just a matter of courtesy: it will get your work known and could lead to further opportunities in the future.

 Maintain a sense of perspective - take a weekend off and come back to it refreshed - especially when you are getting bogged down with details and losing a sense of direction.

 If you are going to panic, don't suffer in silence. Talk to family, friends and tutors. Work out exactly what the problem is, and how to tackle it. Write a plan of action to give yourself control of the situation and work through it.

 Get a friend who is a non-specialist to read your report to see whether it is clear enough.

 Check everything - spelling, punctuation, page layout, typeface, page numbers, etc. - very carefully. If you skimp at the end you will regret it when you see the errors in the final version later.

 Above all, do not lose heart! Many others who have felt the same way have succeeded.

The Final Test

Would the college or university be proud to display your report or dissertation on the library shelves for others to read?

Appendices

Appendix 1
References and Citations

When you quote from, or refer to, another source of information in your report or dissertation, you must provide a citation to it. There are two places where you use a citation:

- at the end of a chapter or section
- in the bibliography towards the end of the report or dissertation.

The aim of a citation is to provide enough bibliographic information for the reader to be able to obtain the original document. Complete, correct and consistent citations are therefore very important.

There are two main systems used in the United Kingdom: the *British Standard (Numeric) system*, and the *Harvard system*. Descriptions of these systems are provided below, together with examples of their use.

There are two main rules for quotations, whichever system you use.

- If you are quoting something that is up to three lines in length then you can generally incorporate this directly into the body of your text; anything longer should be indented in its own paragraph.

- If you need to include any words of your own to help make sense of the quotation, make sure they appear in square brackets to make it clear that these are not part of the quote itself. For example:

"That [moving] line established the efficiency of the method and we now use it everywhere".

Remember that your college or institution may have devised their own referencing and citation system. Ask your tutor or librarian for a house style manual.

British Standard (Numeric) System

Within the text of a report the citation is assigned a number which runs consecutively. This applies where a direct quotation is given:

"A questionnaire is a series of predetermined questions that can be either self-administered, administered by mail, or asked by interviewers."(1)

or where the work is referred to:

... a study on questionnaires (1) provided evidence that ...

In the list at the end of a chapter or section, the references appear sequentially in the order in which they appeared in the text. In the main bibliography the references are listed in alphabetical order by author's surname (see examples on pages 86-88).

When more than two authors are given for an item it is common practice to cite the first author followed by the term '*et al*'.

The information required for books and journal articles using the British Standard system is as follows:

Books

- Author's surname and initials
- Title (underlined or in italics)
- Edition (if not the first)
- Place of publication
- Publisher
- Year of publication.

For example:

Berdie, D. R. *et al. Questionnaire design and use.* 2nd ed. Metuchen, NJ: Scarecrow Press, 1986.

Parts of, or contributions, in a book

- Contributor's surname and initials
- Title followed by 'In:'
- Editor or author of the publication (followed by ed. or eds. if appropriate)
- Title of book (underlined or in italics)
- Edition (if not the first)
- Place of publication
- Publisher
- Year of publication
- Page number/s of the contribution.

For example:

Wheatley, R. Company profile - Pilkington Optronics. In: Harrison, P. and D'Vaz, G. *Business process re-engineering.* Corby: Institute of Management Foundation, 1995, p.25-33.

Journal articles

- Author's surname and initials
- Title of article
- Title of journal (underlined or in italics)
- Volume number
- Part number (in brackets)
- Year of publication
- Page number/s

For example:

Saunders, M. N. K. and Lewis, P. Great ideas and blind alleys: a review of the literature on starting research. *Management Learning,* vol 28 (3), 1997, p.283-299.

Example of a list of references and bibliography

At the end of the chapter or section the references are listed, in the numerical sequence in which they were used. For example:

1. Berdie, D. R. *et al. Questionnaire design and use.* 2nd ed. Metuchen, NJ: Scarecrow Press, 1986.

2. Wheatley, R. Company profile - Pilkington Optronics. In: Harrison, P. and D'Vaz, G. *Business process re-engineering.* Corby: Institute of Management Foundation, 1995, p.25-33.

3. Saunders, M. N. K. and Lewis, P. Great ideas and blind alleys: a review of the literature on starting research. *Management Learning,* vol 28 (3), 1997, p.283-299.

There are some commonly used conventions with the British Standard system for citing references which have occurred more than once in a chapter or section. These are:

- *Ibid.* - used when the same reference from the same source is cited consecutively. For example:

1. Berdie, D. R. *et al. Questionnaire design and use.* 2nd ed. Metuchen, N.J: Scarecrow Press, 1986.
2. *Ibid.*
3. *Ibid.*

- *Op. cit.* - used to refer to the same work last cited for the author. For example:

1. Berdie, D. R. *et al. Questionnaire design and use.* 2nd ed. Metuchen, N.J: Scarecrow Press, 1986.
2. Wheatley, R. Company profile - Pilkington Optronics. In: Harrison, P. and D'Vaz, G. *Business process re-engineering.* Corby: Institute of Management Foundation, 1995, p.25-33.
3. Berdie, D. R. *et al. Op. cit.*

The main bibliography would look like this, with the references in alphabetical order of author's surname:

- Berdie, D. R. *et al. Questionnaire design and use.* 2nd ed. Metuchen, N.J: Scarecrow Press, 1986.

87

Saunders, M. N. K. and Lewis, P. Great ideas and blind alleys: a review of the literature on starting research. *Management Learning,* vol 28 (3), 1997, p.283-299.

Wheatley, R. Company profile - Pilkington Optronics. In: Harrison, P. and D'Vaz, G. *Business process re-engineering.* Corby: Institute of Management Foundation, 1995, p.25-33.

Harvard System

Within the text of a report the Harvard system requires that the author's surname is mentioned and the date of publication of the item. This applies where a direct quote is given:

"A questionnaire is a series of predetermined questions that can be either self-administered, administered by mail, or asked by interviewers." Berdie (1986)

or where a work is referred to:

... a study on questionnaires (Berdie 1986) provided evidence that ...

When more than one publication by the same author, published in the same year, is cited, then lower case letters are used to differentiate the items i.e. (1997a), (1997b). For example:

"A questionnaire is a series of predetermined questions that can be either self-administered, administered by mail, or asked by interviewers." Berdie (1986a)

In cases where more than two authors are responsible for a publication the first author's name is stated, followed by the term '*et al*' (in italics) and the date of publication. For example:

Berdie *et al* (1986) concluded that ...

In the list of the references at the end of a chapter or section, and in your main bibliography, the items are listed alphabetically by author's name (see example on page 91). If an author has been acknowledged more than once with different publication dates, then the items are listed in chronological order, with the earliest item being listed first. The lower case letters used to differentiate publications in the same year are also included in alphabetical order.

The information required for books and journal articles using the Harvard system is as follows:

Books
- Author's surname and initials
- Year of publication
- Title (underlined or in italics)
- Edition (if not the first)
- Place of publication
- Publisher.

For example:

Berdie, D. R. *et al.* (1986) *Questionnaire design and use.* 2nd ed. Metuchen, N.J: Scarecrow Press.

89

Parts of, or contributions, in a book

- Contributor's surname and initials
- Year of publication
- Title followed by 'In:'
- Editor or author of the publication (followed by ed. or eds. if appropriate)
- Title of book (underlined or in italics)
- Edition (if not the first)
- Place of publication
- Publisher
- Page number/s of the contribution.

For example:

Wheatley, R. (1995) Company profile - Pilkington Optronics. In: Harrison, P. and D'Vaz, G. *Business process re-engineering.* Corby: Institute of Management Foundation, p.25-33.

Journal articles

- Author's surname and initials
- Year of publication
- Title of article
- Title of journal (underlined or in italics)
- Volume number
- Part number (in brackets)
- Page number/s

For example:

Saunders, M. N. K. and Lewis, P. (1997) Great ideas and blind alleys: a review of the literature on starting research. *Management Learning,* vol 28 (3), p.283-299.

Example list of references or bibliography

Berdie, D. R. *et al.* (1986) *Questionnaire design and use*. 2nd ed. Metuchen, N.J: Scarecrow Press.

Saunders, M. N. K. and Lewis, P. (1997) Great ideas and blind alleys: a review of the literature on starting research. *Management Learning*, vol 28 (3), p.283-299.

Wheatley, R. (1995) Company profile - Pilkington Optronics. In: Harrison, P. and D'Vaz, G. *Business process re-engineering*. Corby: Institute of Management Foundation, p.25-33.

Further information

There are a number of guides to citing references available on the Internet. Typing in 'citation styles' in any of the major search engines (see Appendix 4) will help you locate them. Remember as well that there are a number of ways for citing Internet references themselves; again style guides are available for these on the Internet. There are a number of books on citing references as well, which give far greater coverage than is possible here, and provide details for referencing more ephemeral items, such as conference proceedings, company reports and electronic media. Ask about these in your college or university library.

Appendix 2
Finding Information on Management

One of the best ways to find information on a specific management subject is to use an abstracting and indexing service. These services provide references and abstracts to a variety of sources, but mainly journal articles. In some cases the full-text of journal articles is also available. You can access them through a library in hardcopy, on CD-ROM and, increasingly, on the Internet.

Institute of Management International Databases (IMID) Plus

Publisher: Institute of Management and Bowker Saur

Six databases containing references and abstracts to over 70,000 items on the theory and practice of management, including books, pamphlets, reports, research papers, journal articles, audiovisual material, and training packages.

ANBAR Management Intelligence

Publisher: MCB University Press

An abstracting service which covers over 400 international journals, and is divided into seven management fields: top management, accounting, personnel, marketing, operations management, information management, and quality.

ABI Inform

Publisher: UMI

Contains over one million abstracts and citations from approximately 1,000 international journals (200 non-American) covering all areas of business, including marketing, strategy, law, finance, economics, accounting, technology, human resources and organisational development. Full-text articles are available from 500 journals.

European Business ASAP

Publisher: Information Access Company

Provides indexing and abstracting for over 900 business, management, economics, industry, and local area business journals. Over 70,000 articles are in full-text.

Helecon CD-Rom International

Publisher: Helsinki School of Economics

Comprises a number of databases with references to international journal articles, books, dissertations, working papers, research reports and conference papers in the fields of business and management. The principal management databases are: SCIMA, which contains abstracted references to articles on various subjects, including management, marketing and economics; and SCANP, the Scandinavian management and economic database of bibliographic references.

UNCOVER

Publisher: B H Blackwell

UnCover is an online table of contents, index and article delivery service for approximately 17,000 magazines and journals, containing about six million articles, to which 5,000 citations are added daily. Searching the index is free but there is a charge for document delivery.

Management and Marketing Abstracts

Publisher: PIRA International

Provides abstracts of articles taken from over 200 management and marketing journals worldwide. An emphasis is placed on practical material, including case studies and company profiles. Subjects covered include general management, finance, personnel, marketing, advertising, corporate strategy and economics.

A far larger number of abstracting and indexing services is detailed in:

- **World databases in management**
  C J Armstrong (ed)
  London   Bowker Saur   1995
  (World database series)
  ISBN: 185739190X   £95.00

TOP *TIP!*

It is rare that one information source, however good, will cover all the information that you need.

Appendix 3
Finding Market and Company Information

Some of the principal sources of market and company information are listed below. Bear in mind that searching for detailed information can prove quite costly but, with a bit of perseverance, a certain amount can be collected at little or no expense.

Market Information

A number of companies specialise in the production of market survey reports. They tend to be very expensive, however. Large public and academic libraries sometimes hold a number of the important ones. **The Business Information Service** at the Science Reference Library has one of the largest collections in the United Kingdom, and is well worth contacting for information. A very useful, and free, quick reference service is available, whereby qualified staff will spend up to 10 minutes dealing with an enquiry.

The address is:

The Business Information Service
25 Southampton Buildings
London
WC2A 1AW
Tel: 0171 412 7454

One of the most useful sources for identifying a market survey is the *Marketing Surveys Index* which provides details of more than 37,000 market reports. It is indexed by subject and updated monthly. The contents and price of each report are given together with the address, telephone and fax number of the publisher.

There are a number of online services which provide a massive amount of information, but a charge will usually be made by a library for searching them. Three good examples of databases holding market information are:

- *PROMT* - includes over three million records of articles and reports with detailed abstracts and summary numeric data. The market information covered includes supply and demand; competition and trade; and capacities. An increasing amount of the information is now full-text.

- *MAID* - a collection of databases providing full-text market research data from over 50,000 reports for international markets. Coverage includes banking and finance; pharmaceuticals and cosmetics; marketing and retail; aerospace and defence; and country reports. Over 450 market sectors are covered.

- *ICC Key Note Research* - includes the full-text of market research reports on over 150 industry sectors published by Key Note Publications Ltd. Reports contain market size and trends, industry structure, major companies, recent developments and forecasts for the future. The majority of reports cover the UK market and some are available with a European overview.

Business Information

Printed Directories

Directories published in book form are easy to locate as they are available in most public reference and college libraries. They cost nothing to consult but the information is not always up-to-date. Examples of such directories and their coverage include:

- *Key British Enterprises (KBE)* - the top 50,000 British companies.

- *Kompass* - 46,000 leading industrial or industrial service companies and more detailed financial information on 30,000 companies.

Information typically given in directories includes the address of the company, telephone and fax numbers, summary financial information, number of employees, principal activities, and the names of directors.

Electronic Databases

Both *KBE* and *Kompass* are available online and on CD-ROM. Most libraries offer an online search service. Some will charge for searches and the most straightforward search will cost at least £30.00.

However, information should be far more detailed and more up-to-date than that from a printed directory. Other company information databases include:

- *ICC British Company Financial Datasheets* - provides financial information, including profit and loss account, balance sheet, business ratios, growth rates, industry comparisons and ICC's recommended credit limit, for all companies with limited liability in the UK.

- *Infocheck UK Company Financial Datasheets* - contains full credit reports and detailed analysis of over 400,000 registered companies, to help provide a picture of a company's trading history, ownership, payment trends, types of borrowing and previous financial problems.

There are also a number of online databases which allow you to search across a wide range of newspapers and journals. These will be useful for commentary information on a company's activities. The two major sources are:

- *Reuters Textline* - contains details of articles, most with full-text, taken from over 600 sources, including major UK newspapers, worldwide press and trade publications. Information is available on companies, industries, economies and countries.

- *FT Profile* - a collection of databases from the Financial Times Group. Files of full-text sources contain information on companies, industries, international business and finance, marketing, advertising and much more.

Annual Reports

Annual reports can be obtained by contacting the company concerned and a copy will sometimes be sent out free of charge. Some business and university libraries maintain a collection of annual reports. One of the largest collections of these and other business information sources is held at the **Science Reference Library** (see page 98).

Companies House

The Cardiff headquarters of Companies House holds the records of over one million companies with a registered office in England or Wales. Information on Scottish companies can also be obtained. Enquiries can be made in person, by telephone or by post.

There are various satellite offices where searches can only be requested by personal visit. The addresses of the headquarters and branch offices of Companies House are:

Companies House - Headquarters
Crown Way
Cardiff
CF4 3UZ
Tel: 01222 380801

Companies House - Scotland
37 Castle Terrace
Edinburgh
EH1 2EB
Tel: 0131 535 5800

Companies House - London Search Room
55-71 City Road
London
EC1Y 1BB
Tel: 0171 253 9393

Companies House - Leeds Search Room
25 Queen Street
Leeds
LS1 2TW
Tel: 0113 233 8338

Companies House - Manchester Search Room
75 Mosley Street
Manchester
M2 2HR
Tel: 0161 236 7500

Companies House - Birmingham Search Room
Central Library
Chamberlain Square
Birmingham
B3 3HQ
Tel: 0121 233 9047

The Press

If you have sufficient time, monitor the business section of the daily press and business publications, such as the Economist. If you are in a hurry, most of the national press now have an Internet presence and some, like the Financial Times, allow you to search their archive free of charge.

Appendix 4
Sources of Information on the Internet

The Internet is a rich (and often free) source of information for people interested in the subject of management. As a student you may find that your college or university provides access to the Internet and an e-mail address through JANET (Joint Academic Network). If your college cannot provide you with these you may consider subscribing to an Internet Access Provider.

We have decided not to provide addresses of web sites or discussion lists in this guide as addresses change and sites appear and disappear overnight. Here are some tips for using the Internet, however.

Locating Relevant Web Sites

1. Use search engines. The following are some of the most popular:

- YAHOO
- ALTAVISTA
- MAGELLAN

- EXCITE
- INFOSEEK
- NETSCAPE

If you want to cut down on the number of possible hits and improve on the relevance of those retrieved:

- use a particular geographic version of the search engine. For example the UK version of *Yahoo!* gives you the option of searching UK sites only.

- choose your search terms carefully by thinking of:
    - alternative meanings of the words you use - you will be surprised how many other applications of the term there can be
    - synonyms, broader and narrower terms
    - the context in which you want to apply the term.

- consider any advanced search capability that the search engine may have, for example:
    - phrase-searching, as well as individual word searching
    - relevance ranking which tells you how many of your search terms are included in each item found
    - AND, OR, NOT operators which enable you to combine, include and exclude terms in your search.

2. Visit sites which specialise in refereeing links to other sites. See, for example, the sites of the University of Nijenrode in the Netherlands and the Institute of Management.

3. Use bookmarks or keep a separate list of web addresses to make it easy to find interesting sites again.

4. Locate electronic journals on management (possibly through printed journals) and scan contents pages for useful articles. This may impress examiners!

Locating Useful Discussion Lists

Professional journals in the management field sometimes give details of lists in their particular specialism. You can retrieve a list of lists in the management field from the Academy of Management or consult *The Directory of Scholarly and Professional Electronic Conferences* by Diane Kovacs. This is published by the United States Association of Research Libraries and is available via the Internet in various forms.

TOP **TIP!**

Make use of e-mail lists to bounce around ideas and search for resources, but don't do it if you are getting hundreds of messages a day. You can't afford the time to deal with them all.

Further Reading

There are many books which provide information about how to use the Internet. You will find a selection of these at your local college, public library or bookshop.

Appendix 5
Professional Associations in the Management Field

Low-cost membership is usually offered to students by professional associations. Check whether the assocation in which you are interested has a library and information service, staffed by qualified researchers. Ask about the size and scope of the association's collection, and the turnaround time for their services. Check out their charges for:

- undertaking a literature search

- supplying books on loan

- providing photocopies of journal articles.

You will also get at least one professional journal and a reduced rate for other publications as well.

The following are the main management associations in the United Kingdom:

- **Institute of Management**
  Management House
  Cottingham Road
  Corby
  Northants
  NN17 1TT

  Tel: 01536 204222
  Fax: 01536 201651
  E-mail: member@inst-mgt.org.uk
  WWW: http://www.inst-mgt.org.uk

  Journals: Management Today and Professional Manager

- **Chartered Institute of Management Accountants**
  63 Portland Place
  London
  W1N 4AB

  Tel: 0171 637 2311
  Fax: 0171 631 5309
  E-mail: pr@cima.org.uk
  WWW: http://www.cima.org.uk/cima/

  Journal: Management Accounting

- **Chartered Institute of Marketing**
  Moor Hall
  Cookham
  Maidenhead
  Berks
  SL6 9QH

  Tel: 01628 852310
  Fax: 01628 850079
  E-mail: membership@cim.co.uk
  WWW: http://www.cim.co.uk

  Journal: Marketing Business

- **Institute of Administrative Management**
  40 Chatsworth Parade
  Petts Wood
  Orpington
  Kent
  BR5 1RW

  Tel: 01689 875555
  Fax: 01689 870891
  E-mail: iadmin@cix.compulink.co.uk
  WWW: http://www.electranet.com/iam

  Journal: British Journal of Administrative Management

- **Institute of Management Services**
  1 Cecil Court
  London Road
  Enfield
  EN2 6DD

Tel: 0181 363 7452
Fax: 0181 367 8149

Journal: Management Services

- **Institute of Personnel and Development**
IPD House
35 Camp Road
London
SW19 4UX

Tel: 0181 971 9000
Fax: 0181 263 3333
E-mail: ipd@ipd.co.uk
WWW: http://www.ipd.co.uk

Journal: People Management

- **Institute for Supervision and Management**
Stowe House
Netherstowe
Lichfield
Staffs
WS13 6TJ

Tel: 01543 251346
Fax: 01543 415804
E-mail: iaea@ismstowe.demon.co.uk

Journal: Modern Management

One of the most useful sources for finding out whether there is a professional association in a particular field is:

- **The Directory of British Associations and Associations in Ireland 1995-96**
  13th edition
  S P A Henderson and *A J W Henderson (eds)*
  Beckenham   CBD Research   1996
  ISBN: 0900246766